MYSTERY HUNTERS

THE WORLD'S STRANGEST UNEXPLAINED MYSTERIES

By John Hawkins

PowerKiDS press.

New York

Published in 2012 by The Rosen Publishing Group, Inc.
29 East 21st Street, New York, NY 10010

Author: John Hawkins
Editor and Picture Researcher: Joe Harris
U.S. Editor: Kara Murray
Design: Emma Randall
Cover Design: Emma Randall

Picture Credits:
Corbis: 9, 27, 28. iStockphoto: 5, 6, 12, 20, 21. Shutterstock: cover, 1, 4, 7, 11, 14, 15, 17, 18, 19, 23, 32.

Library of Congress Cataloging-in-Publication Data

Hawkins, John.
  The world's strangest unexplained mysteries / by John Hawkins. — 1st ed.
      p. cm. — (Mystery hunters)
  Includes index.
  ISBN 978-1-4488-6430-0 (library binding) — ISBN 978-1-4488-6443-0 (pbk.) —
ISBN 978-1-4488-6444-7 (6-pack)
  1. Curiosities and wonders—Juvenile literature. I. Title.
  AG243.H295 2012
  001.94—dc23
                              2011027117

Printed in China
SL002066US

CONTENTS

CROP CIRCLES

The beautiful geometric shapes known as crop circles have been appearing in fields for more than 300 years. Over 5,000 have appeared in more than 40 countries. Many are undoubtedly hoaxes. However, could some be real instances of mysterious forces at work?

▲ Could crop circles be symbolic messages from an alien civilization?

UFOS AND EARTH FORCES

Some witnesses claim to have seen crop circles being made. They say an invisible line snakes at high speed through a field, pushing the stalks of crops aside. When it reaches a certain point, it begins to spin around, pushing the crops down, like the hands on a clock. When it has turned the full 360 degrees, the force vanishes, leaving the crops perfectly matted on the field floor. Tales of UFOs above fields the night before new formations appear are also common.

Many people say crop circles are caused by freak weather conditions, such as tiny whirlwinds. Others say they occur around historic areas of "high natural energy." They point to the fact that they often appear near ancient forts, burial mounds, and

▼ *Crop circles are not always circles. In fact their shapes and patterns vary enormously.*

standing stones, suggesting a connection with humankind's prehistoric culture.

STRANGE EFFECTS?

Video and audio recording devices have reportedly malfunctioned inside crop circles. Farmers have claimed that harvesting equipment fails to work near them. Some people have said they feel improved physical well-being in certain circles, while others have reported feelings of nausea, migraines, and fatigue. Some have seen animals behaving strangely, with horses and cats becoming nervous near patterns and flocks of birds veering around them.

STRANGE STORIES

The Mowing-Devil

The Mowing-Devil is the title of an English pamphlet published in 1678, which is regarded by some as providing one of the first recorded examples of a crop circle. The pamphlet tells of a farmer who was outraged by the price a laborer asked for mowing his field of oats. The farmer exclaimed that he would sooner the Devil mow it. That night the field burst into flames, and the morning after, it was neatly mowed. The pamphlet's illustration shows a crop circle.

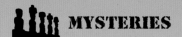

THE BERMUDA TRIANGLE

The Bermuda, or Devil's, Triangle is an area of ocean found off the southeastern tip of the United States. A widespread belief is that countless boats and planes have been inexplicably lost there. It is true that some high-profile disappearances have occurred in the region.

MYSTERY OF FLIGHT 19

The most famous loss in the triangle occurred on December 5, 1945. A squadron of five U.S. Navy Avenger torpedo bombers, known as Flight 19, set off from Florida for the island of Bimini. About an hour and a half into the flight, radio operators received a signal from the commander, Lt. Charles Taylor, saying his compasses weren't working, but he believed he was over the Florida Keys. In fact he

▼ According to popular belief, the Bermuda Triangle has been the site of countless unexplained disappearances over the years.

▲ *One explanation is that magnets do not work normally in the Bermuda Triangle. This causes ships to lose their way.*

THEORIES

All sorts of theories have been put forward to explain the loss of Flight 19 and other high-profile losses in the area. Some say that visiting UFOs enter an underwater base near Bermuda, or that evil marine creatures are responsible, or that the triangle is the site of a gateway to another dimension. Some blame huge clouds of methane gas escaping from the seabed.

NATURAL EXPLANATIONS

The U.S. Coast Guard believes that the losses in the area are caused by bad weather and human error. They say the Bermuda Triangle is no more treacherous than any other waterway.

was over the Bahamas, and the directions he was then given took him further away from land. After that, radio contact was lost and search craft were dispatched. One of the rescue crafts lost communication and another exploded soon after take-off. Flight 19 has never been found.

STRANGE STORIES

The Dragon's Triangle

An area with a similar reputation to the Bermuda Triangle is the Dragon's Triangle, off the west coast of Japan. Japanese sailors call it "Ma no Umi," which means "Sea of the Devil." Some say they've seen red lights and heard terrible noises. There is a legend that a sea monster, Li-Lung, lives there. After numerous losses in the 1940s, the Japanese government dispatched a research vessel, the *Kiao Maru No.5* in 1952, to study the area. It disappeared without a trace.

THE NAZCA LINES

On the arid plateau of the Nazca Desert, in Peru, are some enormous and mysterious markings. Many are in the shape of people, animals, and plants. There are also hundreds of criss-crossing, randomly spaced lines, some forming squares, triangles, and other shapes. One line is over 8.7 miles (14 km) long.

▲ The Nazca Lines are only properly viewable from the air.

AERIAL VIEW

The lines appear to be centuries old, and locals have always known about them. Yet it was only in the 1930s, when regular air travel began in South America, that the truly remarkable nature of these lines was revealed. This is because the pictures and designs can only be appreciated from the air!

WHO CREATED THEM?

The pictures were produced using gravel, soil, and the unusually colored under crust. No one knows who created them because they cannot be dated. However, it is widely believed that they were created by the Nazca, a sophisticated people, skilled in pottery, weaving, and architecture, who lived over 3,000 years ago.

▲ *This aerial view appears to show a spider, one of the animal shapes found in the Nazca Lines.*

ceremonies, or they showed underground sources of water. One theorist even suggests the Nazca were early aviators who developed the world's first hot-air balloon. Another writer, Erich von Daniken, suggested the lines were runways for alien visitors.

WHAT WERE THEY USED FOR?

There are many theories that seek to explain the Nazca Lines. Depending on whom you believe, they are a calendar based on the stars and planets, they were used for religious

Perhaps the most famous theory was put forward by Dr. Maria Reiche. She said that the lines were used as a sun calendar and an observatory for astronomical cycles. The animals, she theorized, were native representations of stellar constellations.

EYEWITNESS TO MYSTERY

CLEANSING WIND

Dr. Maria Reiche explains how the lines have lasted for so long:
"There are extremely strong winds here, even sandstorms, but the sand never deposits over the drawings. On the contrary, the wind has a cleansing effect, taking away all the loose material. This way, the drawings were preserved for thousands of years. It is also one of the driest places on earth, drier than the Sahara. It rains only half an hour every two years!"

THE PIRI REIS MAP

In 1929, a segment of an extraordinary map was unearthed in Istanbul, Turkey. The old gazelle-skin map seems to show part of the Atlantic Ocean and includes the Americas and Antarctica in striking detail.

▲ The Piri Reis map appears to show the outline of Antarctica under the ice.

ACCURATE MAPPING

The strange thing was that the map was created in 1513, only 21 years after Columbus landed in the Americas, and three centuries before Antarctica was discovered. It seems to show the coastline of Antarctica under the ice. The ice is up to 2.5 miles (4 km) thick, and the land under it wasn't mapped until 1949.

The map places the Falkland Islands at the correct latitude, despite the fact that they weren't discovered until 1592, and Greenland is shown as three separate islands, something only discovered in the twenty-first century.

WHO CREATED IT?

The Piri Reis Map is named after its creator, Muhiddin Piri, an admiral (reis) in the navy of Ottoman Turkey. On his travels he collected all kinds of charts of the coastlines and lands in the known world. He used these to compile his 1513 map of the world. The segment of the map that still exists is only a portion of the original.

▼ *Is it possible that someone living in 1513 could have had an accurate knowledge of the Antarctic region?*

MAP THEORIES

Some people believe that an ancient race of humans, using advanced but now lost technology, were able to record the details of Antarctica before it was covered with ice. Others suggest alien creatures mapped the planet, leaving their results behind to be copied by humankind.

EXAMINING THE EVIDENCE

ANTARCTICA—AN INSPIRED GUESS?

Experts point out that many maps from this time included imaginary continents in the South Atlantic, and Piri may just have been lucky with his guesswork. They say that ice has covered Antarctica for hundreds of thousands of years, at least. However, others claim that the continent may have been ice-free as late as 6,000 years ago.

EASTER ISLAND

Easter Island, or Rapa Nui, is a volcanic island in the South Pacific, some 2,286 miles (3,680 km) from Peru. The outside world first came to know of it when a Dutch admiral, Jakob Roggeveen, landed there on Easter Sunday, 1722. Roggeveen was astonished by the enormous stone carved figures around the island. How did they get there? What was their purpose?

MOAI

For more than 1,000 years before this, the people of Rapa Nui had been cut off from the rest of the world. In this period, they erected more than 1,000 of these great statues, or "moai," standing between 12 feet (3.6 m) and 25 feet (7.6 m) high and weighing up to 20 tons (18 t). The largest was nearly 65 feet (20 m) tall and weighs 90 tons (82 t). Many of them stood on stone platforms called "ahus."

▲ These are some of the moai statues of Rapa Nui.

◀ Some moai have red ceremonial hats, which represent their high status.

moved into position on the stone platforms remains a mystery. Some believe that they represent ancestors who guard and protect their clan.

WHEN, HOW, AND WHY?

Where did the islanders come from? Some have suggested they are descended from a Polynesian tribe, while others believe they came from South America. They probably settled on the island in about AD 500 and began building the statues soon afterward. Experts believe the statues were built out of stone from the walls of volcanic craters. How they were

WHAT HAPPENED?

Easter Island was a beautiful, fertile island with plentiful natural resources during the period when the statues were built. But in about AD 1500, overpopulation and poor land management led to crop failure and war. By the 1700s, Easter Island was largely a barren wasteland.

STRANGE STORIES
Statue toppling

After Roggeveen's visit in 1722, the moai were all gradually toppled, with the last one falling in 1868. According to oral histories, this was a result of a conflict among the islanders. Moai were usually toppled forward so their faces were hidden and, often, their necks broke. Today, around 50 moai have been re-erected on their stone platforms or in museums.

THE GREAT PYRAMID

The ancient Egyptians built the pyramids to demonstrate their dead kings' importance and to aid their passage to the afterlife. The greatest of these is the Great Pyramid of Khufu, at Giza. It was built in about 2500 BC in Giza, 10 miles (16 km) south of present-day Cairo.

PRECISE ARCHITECTURE

There are many fascinating aspects of the Great Pyramid's design. Its sides run perfectly north to south and east to west to within a tenth of a degree. The base is an almost exact square, with an error margin of just 6.8 inches (18 cm), and the pavement around the structure is level to within 1 inch (2.5 cm). The Great Pyramid contains a great number of chambers and corridors. One of these, the Ascending Passageway, runs for 344 feet (105 m) directly north.

▲ The Great Pyramid of Khufu (center) is the oldest and largest of the three pyramids at Giza.

▲ For thousands of years, the Sphinx has stood guard in front of the Great Pyramid.

say it is a record of all events, past, present, and future. The passageways are timelines and the intersections are great happenings.

Some mathematicians claim the Great Pyramid demonstrates knowledge of the true value of the number pi. Others claim it was built by alien visitors as a landing beacon for their next visit to Earth.

EMPTY INTERIOR

It is assumed that the Great Pyramid was to be the tomb of Khufu and a storehouse of his treasures, but when the pyramid was opened, nothing was found inside but an empty stone sarcophagus.

OTHER THEORIES

In the absence of hard evidence that the Great Pyramid was a burial place, some alternative theories have been concocted to explain its purpose. Some

? FACT HUNTER

GREAT PYRAMID FACTS

How many builders? About 4,000, plus tens of thousands more manual laborers.

How big and heavy? It is 482 feet (147 m) high, with a base covering 31 acres (12.5 ha). It weighs about 6 million tons (5.4 million t).

How long did it take to build? An estimated 30 years to quarry and assemble.

What's it made of? Two and a half million blocks of limestone.

STONEHENGE

Stonehenge is a circle of standing stones on Salisbury Plain in Wiltshire, England. It was built between 3000 BC and 1900 BC and involved transporting and erecting many large blocks of stone. How such an ancient people could have built such a structure, and why, remains a mystery.

STAGES OF CONSTRUCTION

Stonehenge was built in three stages. The first began in about 3000 BC with the creation of a circular ditch and raised bank around the site. The first rock, called the Heel Stone, was positioned to mark the axis of sunrise at the summer solstice. In about 2000 BC, 82 bluestones, each weighing over 4 tons (3.5 t), were moved 239 miles (382 km) from Wales. They were used to create a double circle inside the site.

▼ The standing stones making up Stonehenge form two rough circles.

▲ *Legend has it that the stones of Stonehenge have healing powers.*

Amazingly, the lintel stones that cap the pillars were actually curved to fit the shape of the circle.

WHAT WAS IT USED FOR?

Stonehenge may have been used as a burial site. Shallow holes, dug during the first stage, contain cremated bones. It may also have been an observatory or giant lunar calendar. Astronomer Gerald S. Hawkins published a book in 1965 in which he claimed that Stonehenge was a kind of prehistoric computer, designed by ancient Britons to calculate upcoming eclipses.

The third phase began in about 1900 BC, when 75 sandstone blocks, known as sarsens, were brought in from Avebury, 20 miles (32 km) away. These stones, weighing 25 tons (23 t) and standing 16 feet (5 m) high were pulled to the site using rollers and ropes. They were then shaped and raised into position.

STRANGE STORIES

Stone circle at Castlerigg

Castlerigg Stone Circle in the Lake District is one of the oldest stone circles in Britain. It was built around 3000 BC and is made up of 38 stones of various heights placed in an oval shape. Unique among stone circles in Britain, it has a rectangular arrangement of stones inside the outer ring. There is also a slight mound in the center. Is this a burial chamber? No one knows, as the site has not been properly excavated. Finds around the site, and the arrangement of stones, suggest it may have been used as an astronomical observatory or center of trade.

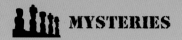
TEOTIHUACÁN

High on a plateau in central Mexico lie the remains of a city that continues to perplex archaeologists and historians. Nobody knows who built it, what they used it for, or why it was abandoned. The remains are awe-inspiring, but it is believed that 90 percent of the city is still buried. At its peak, the city held 200,000 inhabitants. So what happened at Teotihuacán?

A GREAT CITY

The city spread over 7,660 acres (3,100 ha), and its focal point was an immense building called the Pyramid of the Sun. One of the largest buildings in Mesoamerica, it lies at the northern end of a wide road, the Avenue of the Dead, which runs due

▼ *The Pyramid of the Sun at Teotihuacán*

▲ A temple once stood at the summit of the Pyramid of the Sun.

DESTRUCTION

The city shows every sign of having been a wealthy and well-governed society. Yet, for some reason, Teotihuacán was largely destroyed by the eighth century AD. It is possible that the population grew too large for the local resources. More likely, invading barbarians from the north attacked the city. However, it is unlikely that the true story of Teotihuacán will ever be known for certain.

south for 2.8 miles (4.5 km). Near the Pyramid of the Sun is the slightly smaller Pyramid of the Moon. Further south along the Avenue of the Dead is a vast open area called the Citadel, surrounded by temples.

WHO LIVED THERE?

The building of the city began around 200 BC. The major structures were built from the first century AD. The city reached its height of power and population between the fifth and seventh centuries. But who lived there?

? FACT HUNTER

PYRAMID OF THE SUN

How did it get its name? The name was given to it by the Aztecs, who visited Teotihuacán centuries after it was abandoned. The original inhabitants' name for the pyramid is unknown.

How big is it? 733 feet (223 m) across and 234 feet (71 m) high.

What was it used for? It is thought the pyramid was built in honor of a god because a temple (now destroyed) was built on its summit. However, a tunnel and cave discovered beneath the pyramid suggest it may have served as a royal tomb.

KING ARTHUR

According to legend, Arthur was born some time in the fifth century AD. Historians have uncovered several figures with claims to being the true Arthur. But was there ever such a person?

THE ROYAL CHILD

The legend says that Arthur was the illegitimate son of a British king, Uther Pendragon, and Igraine, wife of the Duke of Cornwall. The child was given away at birth, and raised completely unaware of his special lineage. When Uther died, the throne was empty. The magician Merlin set a sword, Excalibur, in rock, and stated that only the true king would be able to remove it.

▲ *The Sword in the Stone could only be released by the true king.*

THE ROUND TABLE

When young Arthur successfully pulled the sword from the stone, he was pronounced king. Eleven other British rulers rebelled against the young leader, but Arthur quashed their uprising and began a noble and glorious reign. Arthur married Guinevere and assembled a group of courageous and noble knights at his court in Camelot in the Vale of

▲ *This engraving shows the great wizard, Merlin, finding Arthur abandoned as a baby.*

rebelled, and Arthur was forced to return home. Arthur fought and defeated Mordred, but he too was killed in the battle.

HISTORY AND LEGEND

The legend may have grown out of an amalgamation (mixture) of the deeds of more than one person. In the sixth century, many Celtic realms had leaders named Arthur, and it's possible that they were all named in homage to a truly inspirational leader who ruled a generation before.

Avalon. They met at the fabled Round Table. The table's shape symbolized equality.

BETRAYED

One of Arthur's most trusted knights, Lancelot, had an affair with Guinevere and fled to Brittany. Arthur followed and waged war on his former friend, leaving his nephew, Mordred, as ruler in his absence. Mordred

EXAMINING THE EVIDENCE
LEGENDARY LEADER

Historical evidence for an Arthurian-type figure can be found in a sixth-century work by Gildas, which refers to British soldiers being led by one Ambrosius Aurelianus. The name Arthur appears in a ninth-century history by Nennius. However, the legend of Arthur really took hold in the twelfth century, with works by William of Malmesbury and Geoffrey of Monmouth.

GHOST SHIP

On November 7, 1872, the *Mary Celeste* left New York with a cargo of alcohol, bound for Italy. On board were the captain, his family, and a crew of seven. On December 4, the crew of another ship spotted the *Mary Celeste* sailing aimlessly ahead of them. The captain sent a boarding party. They found the *Mary Celeste* deserted but in perfectly sailable condition, with good supplies of food and water. Only the navigation equipment and the lifeboat were gone.

▼ *A ship similar to the* Mary Celeste

Alcohol spilled from the cargo barrels, and the ship's movement caused the galley stove to become unstable. Fearing the ship was about to explode, the captain ordered everyone into the lifeboat, planning to follow behind the *Mary Celeste* attached to a rope. But the rope must have snapped and the *Mary Celeste* sailed off, leaving its crew stranded in their small boat.

▲ *What ocean terror could have caused the entire crew to abandon ship?*

WHAT HAPPENED?

One version of events was that the crew had mutinied and then abandoned ship. This seems unlikely as it was a short journey, there were no signs of struggle on board, and the captain was viewed as a decent and respected man. The most probable explanation was that the *Mary Celeste* hit a very bad storm.

? FACT HUNTER

GHOST SHIPS

What are ghost ships? Ghost ships are ships found adrift with the entire crew either missing or dead.

Have there been many ghost ships? Ghost ships were not uncommon during the nineteenth century. The Dutch schooner *Hermania* and the ship *Marathon* were both found abandoned but in perfect working order around the same time as the *Mary Celeste*.

So why is the *Mary Celeste* the most famous ghost ship? The *Mary Celeste* caught the public imagination, mainly thanks to the efforts of *Sherlock Holmes* author Arthur Conan Doyle, who wrote a story about it.

THE SECRET PRINCESS

In July 1918, the Russian Revolution claimed its most famous victims when the czar and his family were executed in Siberia. In 1920, a young woman in Berlin attempted suicide. She was rescued but could not identify herself, so was taken to an insane asylum. In 1922, she began claiming she was the Duchess Anastasia, the youngest daughter of the murdered czar.

▲ Here is Princess Anastasia before the assassination.

ANNA OR ANASTASIA?

The woman, who now called herself Anna Anderson, declared that she had survived the assassination attempt, and one of the soldiers helped her get away. News of her claims soon spread, and she was visited by a number of relatives and acquaintances of the young princess. Anastasia's aunt, Princess Irene, declared her a fraud, but her son Sigismund believed Anna was Anastasia, as did a family friend and the czar's doctor.

▲ *Was this woman a survivor of the massacre of the royal family – or a Polish factory worker?*

A FACTORY WORKER?

One theory suggests that Anna was a Polish woman named Franziska Schanzkowska, a former factory worker who had disappeared in Berlin only a day before Anna was rescued from the canal. Schanzkowska had received similar scars to Anna's from a factory accident. Anna was never able to prove her identity in a court of law. She died of pneumonia in 1984.

STRIKING SIMILARITIES

Anna was similar to the princess in many ways. She spoke excellent English, French, and German. She also had scars on her body that matched her description of her attempted execution. Experts declared that she looked very similar to Anastasia and their handwriting was identical. Anderson was also said to have an amazing knowledge of royal affairs.

EXAMINING THE EVIDENCE

DNA TESTS

The debate over Anna Anderson did not end with her death. In 1991, the remains of the Russian royal family were discovered in Siberia. Scientists compared their DNA with samples of Anderson's hair and found no match. However, Anna did have extremely similar DNA results to blood samples taken from Franziska Schanzkowska's grand nephew. Was the mystery solved? Not quite. When the Russian authorities uncovered the royal corpses, two were missing. One was the czar's son, Alexei. The other was his youngest daughter, Anastasia.

THE IMMORTAL COUNT

The Comte de Saint-Germain was first seen in Venice in 1710. According to witnesses, he looked to be between the ages of 40 and 50. However, people who met him decades later swore he hadn't aged a day. How can this be?

▲ *Is it possible that the Comte de Saint-Germain had slowed his aging by supernatural means?*

MAN OF TALENTS

Throughout his life, according to legend, Saint-Germain looked like a middle-aged man of average height. He had a deep understanding of art and music and created potions that he claimed were the elixir of youth. He was never seen to eat or drink, but he enjoyed socializing with the aristocracy.

SPY AND REVOLUTIONARY

The comte reached the height of his fame in Paris during the 1750s when he acted as a spy for King Louis XV. However, his friendship with the king earned him enemies and he was forced to flee to England. He resurfaced in Russia where he

 If the legend of the comte is to be believed, he may have warned Marie Antoinette about the French Revolution.

apparently played a role in the 1762 revolution.

He next appeared in Paris at the start of Louis XVI's reign, where he supposedly warned Queen Marie Antoinette of a possible revolution. When the king's minister ordered his imprisonment, he disappeared. He sought refuge at the castle of Count Charles of Hesse-Kassel in Schleswig-Holstein, Denmark.

DEATH?

The story goes that by 1784, he had grown weary of life and died. But there is no official record of his death and no tombstone. Some say his death was staged. Certainly, further reports of Saint-Germain were reported. For example, the Countess of d'Adhémar said she met her old friend in 1789, 1815, and 1821, and each time he looked no older than her memory of him.

EXAMINING THE EVIDENCE
WHO WAS HE?

There were many theories about the real identity of the Comte de Saint-Germain, ranging from a Portuguese Jew to the son of the king of Spain's widow. According to a more recent study, he may have been the son of Prince Francis II Rákóczi of Transylvania. One of Prince Francis II Rákóczi's sons apparently died young, but may, in fact, have been raised by a family in San Germano, Italy, hence the comte's name, Saint-Germain.

AN UNCANNY CHILD

On May 26, 1828, a teenage boy stumbled up to the gates of Nuremberg, Germany. A local shoemaker approached him. The boy could barely speak but handed the man an envelope addressed to a captain in the Light Cavalry. Who was he?

▲ This is the house in which Kaspar Hauser was held prisoner.

STRANGE ABILITIES

The letter explained that the boy had been left with a poor laborer who had kept him locked inside all his life, but the boy was now ready to serve in the king's army. The captain questioned the boy, but he had very few words. He could only write the words "Kaspar Hauser," and this became his name. Hauser acted like an infant child. He had no facial expressions, preferred to sleep sitting up, and was happiest in the dark. He also had powerful senses. He could apparently read in the dark, hear whispers from great distances, and identify people by their smell.

CAPTIVE LIFE

The captain placed the boy in the local prison, but the jailer took pity on him and his children began to teach Hauser how to speak, write, and draw. By early 1829, Hauser had learned enough to write his autobiography.

MYSTERIOUS DEATH

In October 1829, a stranger dressed in black came to the house where Hauser was living and tried to murder him. Hauser was moved to the town of Ansbach, Germany. On December 14, 1831, Hauser went to the local park to meet a man who promised to reveal details about his mother. The man attacked Hauser. He died three days later at the age of 21.

▲ *Kaspar Hauser*

He revealed that he had been kept in a tiny cell by a man whose face he never saw. He slept on a straw bed and lived on nothing but bread and water. One day a man came to his cell and taught him to read a little and write his name. The next day, Hauser and the man began a three-day journey that ended with his arrival in Nuremberg.

EXAMINING THE EVIDENCE

WAS HAUSER A BADEN PRINCE?

After Hauser's suspicious death, a rumor began circulating that he was actually a prince, son of Karl of Baden and Stephanie, Grand Duchess of Bavaria. The theory went that Karl's stepmother, the Duchess of Hochberg, switched him at birth with a sickly peasant child. The ill baby soon passed away. Karl himself died young, and on his deathbed claimed he had been poisoned. The throne then passed to his stepbrother, the Duchess of Hochberg's son. It is an unprovable theory.

GLOSSARY

afterlife (AF-ter-lyf) Life after death.

amalgamation (uh-mal-guh-MAY-shun) A combination.

autobiography (ah-toh-by-AH-gruh-fee) An account of a person's life written by that person.

aviator (AY-vee-ay-tur) The pilot of an airplane or other flying machine.

axis (AK-sus) The line around which a body, such as the Earth, rotates.

bluestone (BLOO-stohn) A type of sandstone.

Celtic (KEL-tik) Relating to the group of people who lived in Britain in the time before the Romans.

coastline (KOHST-lyn) The line between the land and the sea.

comte (KONT) A title of French nobility.

constellation (kon-stuh-LAY-shun) A group of stars that have been given a name.

czar (ZAR) An emperor of Russia before 1917.

DNA (dee-en-AY) DNA (deoxyribonucleic acid) is the material that carries an organism's genetic information. Samples of DNA can be used to establish identity.

eclipse (ih-KLIPS) An obscuring of the light from a celestial body by the passage of another body between it and the observer.

geometric (jee-uh-MEH-trik) Relating to geometry, the branch of mathematics concerned with points, lines, surfaces, and solids.

hoax (HOHKS) A deception.

homage (AH-mij) Special honor or respect shown publicly.

illegitimate (ih-leh-JIH-teh-met) An old-fashioned term describing a child born to parents who aren't married to each other.

lineage (LYN-ee-ij) Descent from an ancestor.

lintel (LYN-til) A horizontal support across the top of a door, window, or other type of opening.

Mesoamerica (meh-zoh-uh-MER-uh-kuh) The central region of the Americas, where a number of civilizations flourished before the Spanish colonization of the Americas in the sixteenth century.

observatory (ub-ZUR-vuh-tor-ee) A place used to study natural phenomena, such as the stars.

pi (PY) The circumference of a circle divided by its diameter (approximately 3.14159).

plateau (pla-TOH) An area of relatively level high ground.

prehistoric (pree-his-TOR-ik) The time before recorded history.

Russian Revolution (RUSH-in reh-vuh-LOO-shun) The revolution in the Russian empire in 1917, in which the czar's regime was overthrown.

sarcophagus (sar-KAH-fuh-gus) A stone coffin.

schooner (SKOO-ner) A type of sailing ship with two or more masts.

summer solstice (SUH-mer SOHL-stis) The time when the sun reaches its highest point in the sky at noon, marked by the longest day. The summer solstice marks the onset of summer.

treacherous (TREH-chuh-rus) Dangerous.

FURTHER READING

Burns, Jan. *Crop Circles*. Mysterious Encounters. San Diego, CA: KidHaven Press, 2008.

Rooney, Anne. *Strange Places*. Amazing Mysteries. Philadelphia, PA: W.B. Saunders, 2011.

Walker, Kathryn. *Mysteries of the Ancients*. Unsolved!. New York: Crabtree Publishing, 2009.

Walker, Kathryn. *Mysteries of the Bermuda Triangle*. Unsolved!. New York: Crabtree Publishing, 2009.

WEB SITES

Due to the changing nature of Internet links, PowerKids Press has developed an online list of Web sites related to the subject of this book. This site is updated regularly. Please use this link to access the list:

www.powerkidslinks.com/mysthunt/strange/

INDEX